Tidbits

Tidbits

light verse & observations

Judy DiGregorio

CELTIC CAT PUBLISHING
Knoxville, Tennessee
2015

Tidbits: light verse & observations / Judy Lockhart
DiGregorio
Illustrated by Brandon Daniel

ISBN: 978-0-9905945-8-1

Celtic Cat Publishing
Knoxville, Tennessee
CelticCatPublishing.com

PCN: 2015941683

Printed in the United States of America
Sustainable Forestry Initiative® Certified
Sourcing

Contents

For Dan,
My first and last husband,
With love,
Judy

A day without laughter is a day wasted.

Charlie Chaplin

Wishful Shrinking

"Be careful about reading health books. You may die of a misprint."

Mark Twain

Health, Fitness, Waistlines

Each New Year's Day I make the same resolution – exercise more, eat less, and lose weight, especially those uninvited pounds that have bonded with my body over the holidays. Not only do I long to lose weight, but I crave the tiny waistline I sported as a teenager, even though I recognize this is unrealistic.

To kickstart my resolution, I have pursued different physical activities. In my younger days, I played coed volleyball, basketball, and softball, but my knees eventually begged me to navigate toward other kinder, gentler forms of exercise.

For their sake, I decided to try the cross trainer and other machines at the fitness club. Unfamiliar with the cross trainer, I initially pedaled backwards. When someone pointed it out to me, I was embarrassed to confess I'd never been on one before so I told them that's how I warmed up.

I also attempted Pilates to strengthen the core muscles in my abdominals and back and took classes in Tai Chi, a soft style martial art and low impact exercise program credited with improving circulation, posture, and balance. Pilates and Tai Chi were certainly beneficial to my body, although they did not help me lose weight. I am also a lifetime members of Weightwatchers International so I understand how to count calories and watch what I eat. I understand it, but I don't necessarily do it.

Another method I have tried for staying in shape and losing weight is to perform in musicals at the Oak Ridge Playhouse. This activity sharpens my mind and works out my body. I completed 15 shows of "Cinderella" as a member of the ensemble which played a key role in the production, adding sparkle and interest to the show. In addition to singing, the ensemble danced gavottes and waltzes and skipped in circles around Lionel, the King's servant, in "The Prince Is Giving a Ball."

This spirited number required coordinated stage movements with curtseys, bows, and crosses back and forth across the stage as we carried unwieldy baskets of flowers, fruits and vegetables and/or over-sized trays of meat, cheese, or pastries. Although the pieces of fake fruit, etc., were more or less glued into the baskets, occasional lemons and oranges escaped and rolled haphazardly across the stage. One evening I spotted a loose lemon rolling my way. I had no time to move so I straddled my legs and allowed the lemon to roll between them. Then I finished the dance. The gavotte also encountered problems. Dressed in sky blue evening gowns with poufy crinolines underneath, the ladies in the gavotte ensemble projected elegance and grace as they danced. One night a crinoline suddenly fell off mid-dance. Its owner kicked it aside and continued dancing as the crinoline sat on the stage by itself as different couples collided with it. Someone finally kicked it off into the wings.

Happily, I lost a few pounds doing "Cinderella" and kept myself in good condition due to all the physical action required. However, some things did not change. Remember the Kingston trio song about Charlie who got stuck on the Boston MTA and never returned? Neither did my waistline.

Unsuccessful

I tried to be a golfer,
Fulfillment did I seek,
My spirit was quite willing,
Too bad my swing was weak.

I tried to learn to snorkel,
Did all the things I ought-er,
Slapped on my mask, attached my tube
But all I breathed was water.

I tried to do Pilates
To improve my core,
Laid on my back, stuck up my legs
Then couldn't get off the floor.

HELP!

Point of View

The pudgy hippopotamus
Weighs more than quite a lot of us.
We look quite thin
Compared to him.
He's probably glad he's not of us.

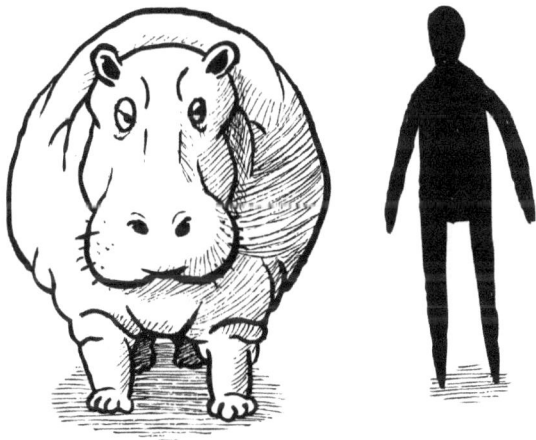

New Location

My waist has disappeared,
I don't know where it went,
But when I pass a mirror,
I see where it was sent.

Diet

Those who bulge
Should not indulge,
Grin and bear it.
Eat a carrot.

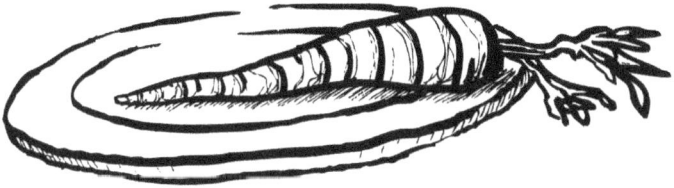

No Solution

Mascara for my eyes,
Powder for my nose,
Lipstick for my lips,
Polish for my toes,

Blusher for my cheeks,
Concealer for my skin,
None of these aids help me
In my efforts to look thin.

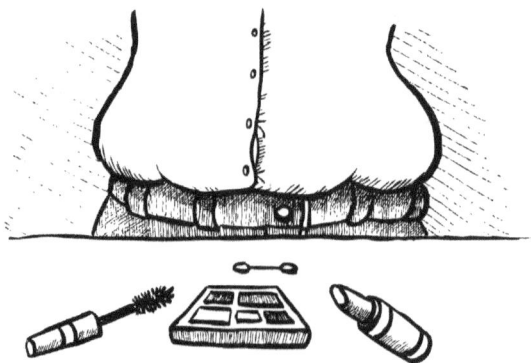

Life Changes

My hair has turned silver
And my scalp has turned pink.
I look in the mirror
And don't know what to think
Hairs on my chin,
A wart on my nose,
Once you reach 50,
Everything goes.

Save Me From Technology

"Do you realize if it hadn't been for Edison
we'd be watching TV by candlelight?"

Al Boliska

The Alien in the iPhone

Several years ago, my husband Dan insisted on giving me a cell phone, even though I did not want one. I fully support new technology, but I don't want to use it. It makes me uneasy and nervous. I'm afraid of making drastic mistakes that cannot be undone.

Over time, I did learn to use the cell phone, a Samsung Convoy sturdy as a Sherman tank, and began to appreciate it. After we dropped our land line, the cell phone became a necessity, not a luxury. Unfortunately, my ancient cell phone died peacefully a few weeks ago. The screen faded to black. Distraught, I cradled it as it shook with its last vibrations. I loved that old phone. I understood it. I trusted it. I knew how to operate it.

To assuage my grief, Dan convinced me to try out an iPhone. The first few days I was completely stressed out. The iPhone possessed alien-like qualities. It did strange things. It made suspicious sounds. I dialed and/or face-timcd half the people on my contacts list by accident. I have never communicated with so many people in such a short time. I'm still not sure how it happened.

I became acquainted with Siri, although we are not yet close friends. Since I already knew how to text, I used Siri's microphone to send text messages instead of typing them. But the microphone sometimes distorted the messages. Dan received one saying I was bringing a Big Ed pizza to the "outhouse" instead of "our house." My daughter Candie got one saying "Siam home" instead of "I am home," reminding me of my old church camp days when we repeated silly chants such as "Owa tagoo siam."

The scariest experience was the day the apps and icons on the screen expanded so big I could not see the phone icon. I knew some demon had invaded the phone, but I didn't know how to remove it. When I returned home, I told Dan about the problem.

"That's nothing," he said. "Tap the screen twice with three fingers, and it will return to normal." "What kind of hocus pocus is this," I asked as I tried it. It didn't work. "Not two fingers, three fingers," Dan repeated, tapping three fingers on the table to demonstrate. I tried again. It still didn't work. Growing impatient, Dan said "Tap it two times, TWO times!" Finally, I did it correctly and thanked Dan for coming to my rescue.

I am still intimidated by my new iPhone and have much more to learn before I am proficient, but I become a little more acclimated every day. However, if you get unexpected calls or facetime requests from me in the middle of the night, please ignore them. I am not calling. It's the insomniac alien inside my iPhone.

Out of Touch

There's nothing like a cellular phone
To help one keep in touch;
But when I see my monthly bill,
I know I've touched too much.

Ups and Downs

I use my email on the days
It works as it's supposed to;
But when I see my system's down,
I wonder why I chose to!

Reality TV

"Dancing with the Stars"
Listening to "The Voice,"
Reality TV
Does not make me rejoice.

Lost

It really is a pity
When I visit a new city
That I lack the homing instincts
Of a pigeon;
Led blindly by my feet,
I wander down each street
But where I go,
I do not know a smidgin.

Arriving at Destination

By nature I am not a suspicious woman, but I have never met a GPS I trust. Most of my friends and family members use a GPS, but as far as I can tell, they don't get anywhere faster or quicker than I do using Map It on the computer or (*GASP!*) an antique fold-out map.

Last year a friend and I headed for Chesapeake's Restaurant in Knoxville for lunch. I knew approximately where it was but couldn't remember the exact location. "No problem," my friend reassured me, "Let me plug in my GPS, and we'll find it in no time."

She added the address, 500 Henley Street, to her GPS which began spitting out commands in a firm female voice reminiscent of a third grade teacher. After a few turns, the intonations changed to "Stay on route." Suddenly in the middle of Henley Street we heard "Arriving at destination." Looking around we caught sight of part of Chesapeake's on the other side of a high wall. However, there was no way to access the restaurant without leaving the car in the middle of Henley Street and climbing over the barrier. We ignored the directions from the frustrated GPS as we navigated through several busy city streets and finally arrived at the restaurant.

My husband Dan uses his GPS and believes everything she says. We recently made a quick trip to Litchfield Beach in South Carolina. We no sooner left the driveway than Miss GPS said "In 500 feet turn right. Turn right."

"Why is she saying 'right' when we're supposed to turn 'left' Dan?"

"She knows what's she doing. You have to trust her," Dan responded.

"Well, whoop dee dee," I thought, "trust her while we go around in circles?"

Once we hit the interstate, Miss GPS was accurate most of the time. Her favorite incantation was "Continue on route." Trouble surfaced when an accident on I-26 closed the interstate and forced us to take a long detour. Miss GPS had a nervous breakdown. On the long and winding road we took, she couldn't decide which direction to give us to steer us back to the interstate. "In one mile, turn right." No road ever appeared. "In one-half mile turn left." Where? Into the bushes? "In 300 feet merge right." Merge how? It's a two-lane road!

After losing about two hours on the detour, we finally arrived on Pawley's Island and began to search for the Litchfield Beach and Golf Resort. We passed Litchfield Racquet Club, Litchfield by the Sea, Litchfield Country Club, and Litchfield Beach Vacation Rentals.

Every time I saw the word Litchfield, I yelled "There it is, Dan. Why isn't the GPS telling us to stop?"

"Because we're not there!" he growled.

Just when I had given up all hope, Miss GPS uttered those magic words "Arriving at destination." Thankfully, this time we really were at our destination.

For those of you who continue to use a GPS, best of luck. GPS stands for Global Positioning System, but it should be renamed *Global Positioning Sometimes.*

Stay Put

When I travel, I unravel
Like a piece of yarn.
I lose my brush, misplace my shoe,
That's bigger than a barn.

There really is no help for it
No matter where I roam,
One solution do I see,
And that's to stay at home.

Old Car, New Car, Gray Car, Blue Car

The older I grow, the more I hate to say good-bye, even if it's to an old family car. When someone accidentally smashed into my nine-year old Mazda gray minivan, it had ferried countless passengers to football games, track meets, and family outings including trips to the sun-kissed sands of Kiawah Island in South Carolina. As comfortable as an old faded robe, the van was steadfast and dependable in all kinds of weather. It was not cool or sporty looking, but it felt like home.

After the collision the front end of my van looked like a giant metal accordion, and the insurance company totaled the vehicle. Saddened, Dan and I bid our old friend a fond farewell and reluctantly tackled the tedious process of buying a new car.

Our insurance covered a rental car for a short time, and we were given use of a Hyundai Genesis, a premium luxury sedan. The rental car attendant handed us something called a fob, told us how much we would love the rental, and left Dan and me sitting in the car on soft tan leather seats. We gazed at a dashboard system worthy of the space shuttle. The fob lay on the seat between us. We stared at it. We stared at the dashboard. We stared at each other. "Dan," I said, "how the heck do you start this thing?" Neither of us had a clue. Finally, we called the attendant back who lectured us on fobs and keyless entry. Then he demonstrated how to put the car in park, press the brake, and push the button on the dash. We felt like idiots as we drove away.

The next two weeks we meandered like no-mads in the desert from one car dealership to the other, hopelessly confused about what we wanted or didn't want. After test driving several cars, we finally purchased a Honda CR-V in a beautiful blue color called Mountain Air Metallic. The CR-V offers many more options than our old van did. We now have a rear view camera, Bluetooth, an Econ button to help maximize fuel economy, an outside temperature sensor, a compass, and perhaps other gadgets we haven't noticed yet.

We still miss the minivan, but we are enjoying driving a sporty new car around, even if we have not conquered all the new technology that goes with it. By the time I am comfortable with this car, we will probably have to buy another. Maybe the next one will brush our teeth for us.

Looks Aren't Everything

"I base my fashion taste on what doesn't itch."

Gilda Radner

Out of Style

Fashion is in, but I am out.
Haute couture, what's that about?
When skirts are long, I trip and fall;
I've hardly any style at all.

Don't wear Prada or Cassini
Won't see me in a string bikini;
Don't be offended if this seems rude
But my best style seems to be nude.

Funny Bone

Elbows are angular,
pointed, and bony.
They often resemble
uncooked macaroni.
They stick out and bump
each sharp
corner and door.
I am so glad
I have
two and
no more,
For elbows
are needed
though we
sometimes must
mend 'em.
It helps
to remember
to
occasionally
bend 'em.

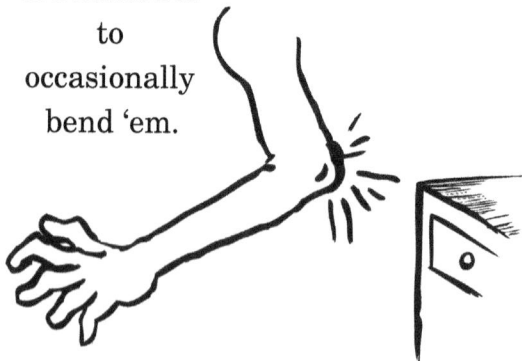

Who Rules?

I think that I shall never see
A bone as brittle as my knee.
It pops and snaps and locks up tight.
It aches and pains me through the night.

As stiff as any board I've seen,
My knee rules o'er me like a queen.
With humbleness, I must kowtow;
I cannot kneel so I just bow.

Diagnosis

Allergies make me sneeze;
Springtime do I dread;
There's nothing wrong with me I'm told;
It's only in my head.

Catchoo

Long-haired or short-haired,
Gentleman or dame,
No matter which cat I encounter,
I sneeze just the same.

Evolution?

Why, I asked my mother,
Do I wear a size 12 shoe?
Was one of our late ancestors
Perhaps part kangaroo?

Tattoos

Tattoos work for the young
Whose skin is still elastic.
On aging skin that has grown thin,
Tattoos don't look fantastic.

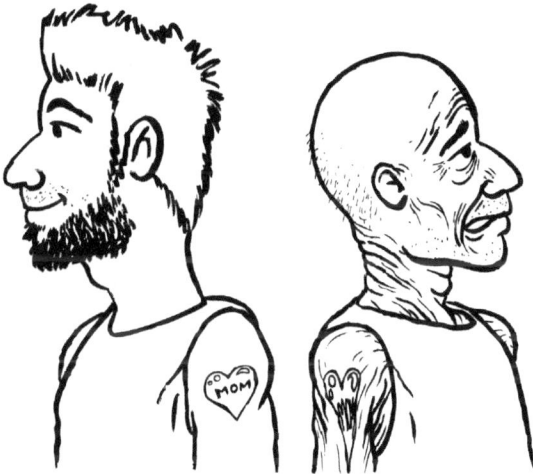

Whatshername

Call me by name
And I'm thrilled that you know it,
But forget who I am,
And, boy, did you blow it.

Mistaken Identity

When I heard my daughter's words,
I thought I'd surely kill her;
I hastened to correct her;
My hair's not gray; it's silver!

First Class

Compare me to a vintage wine,
A chardonnay or such,
But don't announce my year of birth,
'Cause then you've said too much.

Food and Family Bits

"After a good dinner one can forgive anybody,
even one's own relations."

Oscar Wilde

Salad Matters

In our house cooking the Thanksgiving meal is a shared responsibility because I am a minimalist. I do minimal shopping, minimal food preparation, and minimal cooking. Thank heaven, my husband Dan loves to prepare the turkey and dressing. I deal with everything else, including the salad. However, sometimes Dan and I do not agree on how to prepare the salad. My spouse believes the smaller the size of the ingredients, the tastier the salad. Here's our conversation:

ME: Why is this bowl full of green oatmeal?

HIM: That's not oatmeal, that's our salad.

ME: What are these black specks? Pepper?

HIM: Diced black olives.

ME: What about this slimy green stuff?

HIM: Bell peppers and green onions. I threw them into the blender a few minutes.

ME: And I guess the green splotches on the side of the bowl are pieces of lettuce?

HIM: Right. See how much easier it is to eat salad when you chop things up?

ME: We don't even need our salad fork to eat it. A soup spoon will do.

My salad is a little different. I grab a head of iceberg lettuce, rinse it off, and rip it apart with my hands. I lay the leaves in a bowl to which I add a few baby carrots and maybe some cherry tomatoes. This conversation accompanies my salad:

HIM: Can't you cut up the carrots instead of sticking whole ones in the salad?

ME: Why cut them up? It's difficult to stab small pieces of raw carrot with a fork. Besides, everyone knows that the more you chew your food, the better it is for your digestive system. That's why I leave everything in such big portions. I want to keep us healthy.

HIM: If you worried about eating healthy, you wouldn't serve mashed potatoes and gravy, hot buttered yeast rolls, and pecan pie. You just don't like to chop things up. I'm surprised you don't place a whole head of lettuce on a plate and tell everyone to take a bite of it as they pass it around.

I admit I do hate to chop up things, but if you have to use a magnifying glass to identify what's in the salad, you should serve it in a laboratory. Still, no matter who makes the salad, we partake ravenously of the feast and savor each mouthful of food because it's not the turkey, or the stuffing, or the salad that makes Thanksgiving special. It's sharing it with those you love, even if they don't prepare salad the same way you do.

Pasta

Macaroni, rigatoni,
Served with sauce and cheese,
Cooked al dente, an even-te
Sure to make me pleased.

Unappreciated

The lowly pinto bean
Is just a plain legume,
But how its power expands
The more we do consume.

Unnoticed

I went to a banquet
Feeling chic and slim,
Sat at the head table
Where a seed stuck to my chin.
Back home I quizzed my husband
Who answered with a snort.
"Don't blame that on me," said he,
"I thought it was a wart."

Just Shut Up

I'm not a morning person,
So I don't speak 'till noon.
If you feel like talking,
Please kindly leave the room.

Enough

Suddenly the crying stopped;
His sobs were heard no more;
She released the old golf bag
And booted him out the door.

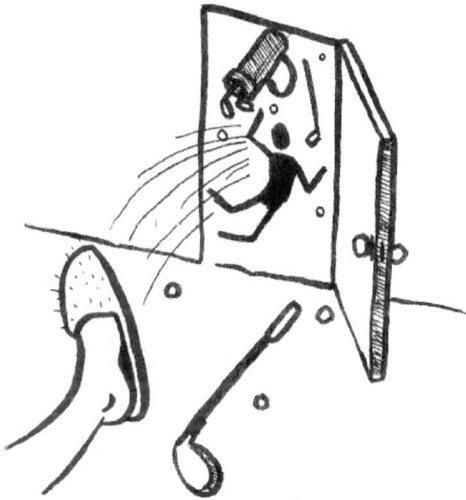

Get Real

Please buy me a diamond, dear,
And I won't complain or moan-ia.
Just slip it on my finger,
And swear it's not zircon-ia.

Please Don't Help

You think you know a person, and then you discover the ugly truth. You do.

After fifty years of marriage, I know my husband Dan pretty well so I should have realized he ignored my words that Saturday morning.

"Dan, I'm washing my bras on the delicate cycle. I'll hang them up when I come back from shopping. Whatever you do, do not put them in the dryer."

A decent bra costs between $25 and $30. Multiply this by a factor of seven, one for each day of the week, and the cost increases considerably. That's why I treat my bras with tenderness and respect.

I returned later to find Dan gone and a groaning noise coming from the dryer downstairs. My bras had finished their delicate cycle hours ago so I thought Dan must have emptied the washer and decided to do some of the other laundry piled next to it.

I rushed downstairs to the garage and saw no bras hanging anywhere. This could mean only one thing. Undoubtedly, they were disintegrating in the clothes drier.

Dan is democratic about the laundry. In his eyes, everything is equal. Rugs, jeans, sweatshirts, silk blouses, or bras are indistinguishable to him. It doesn't matter what color they are, what weight they are, or what material they are. In his universe, they are one. They are washed, dried, and faded together.

I took a tentative step toward the dryer that stood before me like a porcelain idol awaiting more sacrifices of wet laundry. Bravely, I yanked the door open. The heat assaulted me like a Santa Ana wind as my eyes widened at the huge mountain of clothing.

Dan must have set the dryer timer on the longest setting of two hours to sterilize the clothes as well as dry them. After a few minutes, I reached in, retrieved the laundry, and shoved it into a sturdy plastic basket. Then I staggered up the stairs, dumped it onto my king-size bed, and began to pull items apart.

The first object smelled like burnt rubber and appeared to be the remains of a blue bathroom rug. I found some pink pillowcases and sheets along with a faded red sweatshirt.

Finally, I saw bits of embroidered satin and shriveled pieces of black netting, remnants of the Victoria's Secret bra I had splurged on to wear under a special party dress. Then I discovered the skeletal remains of more bras. They had melted together into the form of an octopus with mangled straps dangling from the body like tentacles.

When Dan finally returned, I showed him the results of the dryer marathon and pointed to the pitiful stack of bras. Shamefacedly, he hung his head and uttered those infamous words spoken by every man who knows he's done wrong.

"I was only trying to help."

"I'm sure you were, dear," I replied, "but we can't afford any more of your help in this area. Now repeat after me:

It's OK to do my laundry.
It's OK to do my duty.
It's OK to wash my own clothes.

But don't try to help Judy."

Get-up Time

(with apologies to Robert Louis Stevenson)

I have a little grandson
Who climbs in and out with me.
He's in my bed before it's dawn,
His face alight with glee.

He pokes me, and he pats me,
Get-up time, he shouts;
I feebly try to hold him still
While his legs thrash about.

And as I slowly move my lips,
His arms clutch my neck tight;
Please go to sleep, I beg of him;
It isn't even light.

How 'bout I sing a song, he says,
Or maybe find the cat?
My tummy's really hungry, Grams;
Where's my breakfast at?

I finally stumble out of bed,
And down the hall we creep;
I really love grand-mothering,
But what I miss is sleep!

Tarantulas and Birthdays

"Do you think they put the tarantula back in its cage, Grandma," a small voice whispered.

I opened one eye and stared into my six-year-old grandson's face pressed nose to nose against mine. His arms clutched my neck. The dim glow of a night-light reflected a row of sleeping bags with tousled heads sticking out the tops. As a treat for his birthday, we were spending the night in a cabin at the zoo as part of the "Bedtime with the Beasts" program.

The zoo brochure promised moonlight tours and animal encounters. Tailen and I both looked forward to the adventure. After our group of eight checked in on Friday evening, the two guides gave us a short orientation.

We began the moonlight tour of the zoo when it was pitch dark—but there was no moonlight. Rain was pouring down so we donned our ponchos. Only the guides were allowed to use flashlights because too many lights disturbed the animals. The night was so black that we couldn't see our hands in front of our faces.

We cautiously tripped along a dirt road lined with trees and bushes on our way to the main zoo area. A low-hanging branch slapped me in the face, and I stepped into several puddles and potholes. Rain pelted us from every direction. Soon the only dry spot on my body was my left tonsil. My grandson's night vision was considerably better than mine so he did not fall into any mud puddles. He jumped into them on purpose.

The guides lectured on various exhibits as we slopped along, but we saw no animals. They had enough sense to stay out of the rain and snore peacefully in their dry cages. Due to the persistent downpour, the guides gave up on the night tour. We splashed back to the cabin for an indoor program. By now it was 9 P.M. and I longed for a soft, warm bed.

We shook ourselves like wet dogs as we removed our ponchos and muddy shoes. Then we gathered in a circle on the rug. The guides took turns retrieving animals for our hands-on encounters. They brought out a silky-soft chinchilla, a prickly hedgehog rolled into a little ball, a hissing cockroach, a screech owl, a snake, a large bull frog, and a gecko. The last beast of the evening was the tarantula. It looked scary, but we lightly touched its fuzzy back. Tailen was ecstatic with each new creature he met.

Finally, at 11 P.M. we collapsed onto our sleeping bags and drifted off to the sound of the lions roaring in the distance. I don't know how many times Tailen woke me to ask about the tarantula, but it was not a restful night.

We arose at 7 A.M for a breakfast of muffins and cereal, then went for an early morning tour in the sunshine with the cool air smelling of honeysuckle. The animals were standing near the front of their cages awaiting their breakfast so this time we saw all of them. They looked alert and well-rested. I did not. "Bedtime with the Beasts" was a worthwhile and special way to celebrate Tailen's 6th birthday. But I'm glad he did not ask to do it again for his 7th.

Who's My Muse?

"Be obscure clearly."

E. B. White

Opinion

Writers speak their truths
On the human condition,
Opinions, points of view
Expressed without contrition.

Where's the Proof?

There once was a writer named Shakespeare
Who amazed everyone with his wit;
He wrote verse; he wrote prose
But nobody knows
For sure if he really did it.

Iambic Pentameter

If you write in iambic pentameter,
Don't worry about the parameter.
Just count one to five,
There's no need to jive,
We'll know that you are no amateur.

Not a Brain

A thesaurus is a source of words
A writer likes to use;
Its comprehensive lists and such
Help activate my muse.

The number and variety
Of words can make me blink.
Alas, no shortcut have I found;
I'm still required to think.

Intellectual

I'd rather be clever than dumb,
But the wit that I seek just won't come;
I think and I think
Till I feel on the brink,
But the words that pop out are 'ho hum.'

Great Musicians

Mozart, Rossini, and Bach
Wrote opera and fugues but not rock,
Their music unrated,
Sometimes syncopated,
Hickory dickory dock.

The Pianist

There once was a lady named Jean
Whose demeanor was kind and not mean.
She tickled the keys
Without using her knees
Though her fingers were seldom seen.

The Voice

Coloraturas trill high,
Altos sing low,
Mezzos warble in-between
Where those two don't go.

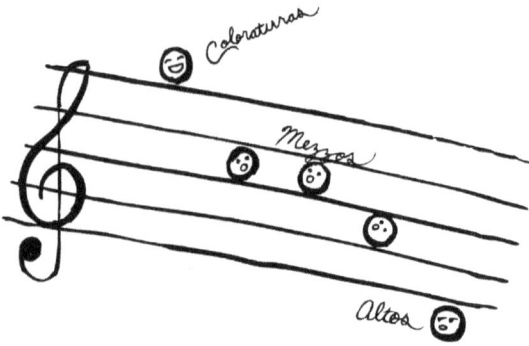

Not a Diva

A singer got stung by a bee,
The result was exciting to see,
She belted, she roared,
She screamed, and she soared,
But the notes that emerged were off key.

Is Bigger Better?

Facilitate, communicate,
Such words make me balk;
Surely there's a simpler way;
Why don't we say "let's talk?"

Last Day

Wall pounding, door slamming,
Rejoicing, hectic sounds,
School is joyous this last day,
Especially in the teachers' lounge.

The Procrastination Predicament

When I have less than 24 hours left to meet a writing deadline, I am as jumpy as a kangaroo rat in a room full of cats. Ideas tumble around in my head like bingo balls in a metal cage as I mentally kick myself for procrastinating again.

I don't procrastinate quite as much in the winter as I do in the spring when blue skies and balmy breezes tempt me to take long walks at the marina where I can watch the great blue heron fishing along the bank or the rowers skimming across the lake. I also enjoy sitting on my deck observing the nuthatches, chickadees, and goldfinches. The only thing I don't enjoy this time of year is parking myself at the computer and writing.

Part of my problem is I write over 50 columns per year so a deadline dangles in front of me almost every week. If I didn't have deadlines to motivate me, I don't know if I'd ever write anything. But deadlines don't prevent me from procrastinating.

I keep notebooks in my house and purse where I jot down possible ideas for columns. I also scribble things on stray pieces of paper such as napkins, Kleenex, or the church bulletin if a notebook is not handy. Of course, those little wisps and bits of paper usually crawl away ending up on the floor where they lurk unnoticed.

When I review any notes I can find, a new problem surfaces. I can't read them. My handwriting has steadily deteriorated since I started using a computer. Every other word I write looks like chicken scratches or hieroglyphics. I might as well be writing prescriptions for a pharmacy. Even the grocery lists I give to my husband require observation, interpretation, and translation.

When I have plenty of time before a column is due, I choose a few ideas to investigate. Each idea gets three paragraphs to test its appropriateness for a full-fledged column. If words do not flow easily or the topic fails to retain my interest, I scrap the idea and try the next one. Using this system I can flesh out a first draft in a few hours and review and edit it for several days before I send it in.

If I wait until the night before the column is due, I grab onto any idea I can find and frantically start crafting a possible column.

Ill-tempered and cranky, I sit hunched over the computer typing and rewriting until the wee hours of the morning. I have never yet missed a deadline, but I have missed many a good night's sleep. Once the column is on its way, I chastise myself for waiting so long and vow not to do it again.

Of course, my resolution to stop procrastinating does not last. Resolutions are similar to the glass in fire alarms. They are meant to be broken.

Acknowledgements

Grateful acknowledgement is made to the following publications in which some of the light verse and essays in this book have appeared.

- *ByLine Magazine*
- *New Millennium Writings*
- *Eva Mag*
- *For Better or Worse Newsletter*
- *East Tennessee Writer*
- *Anderson County Visions Magazine*
- *Putnam County Visions Magazine*
- *Inscriptions Magazine*
- *Our Senior Times*
- *Life among the Lilliputians*
- *Memories of a Loose Woman*

About the Author

Judy DiGregorio, an award winning humor writer, is recognized as a Distinguished Alumna by New Mexico Highlands University and as a Woman of Distinction in the Arts by the YWCA. She writes monthly humor columns for *Anderson County Visions Magazine* and *Putnam County Visions Magazine*. She also writes press releases for the Oak Ridge Playhouse, where she frequently appears on stage. Her work has appeared in the *Chicken Soup* books, *Byline Magazine, CC Motorcycle News Magazine, The Writer, The Army Times, CityView, New Millennium Writings, Knoxville News Sentinel, The Oak Ridger, The Oak Ridge Observer, Oak Ridge Today, Ridges Magazine, Muscadine Lines, Long Story Short, The Tennessee Writer, Southern Hospitality Magazine, The Writing Parent, East Tennessee*

Episcopalian, *The Church Musician Today*, and numerous anthologies. Judy lives in Oak Ridge, Tennessee, with her husband Dan and their cat Noel, who never stops shedding. Visit her website at http://judyjabber.com/.